Original title:
The Light of the Lanternfish

Copyright © 2025 Creative Arts Management OÜ
All rights reserved.

Author: Julian Prescott
ISBN HARDBACK: 978-1-80587-253-5
ISBN PAPERBACK: 978-1-80587-723-3

Sirens of the Dazzling Deep

In the ocean blue, fish do a jig,
Spinning and twirling, dancing so big.
With glows on their tails, they summon the crew,
But stumble on seaweed, oh what a view!

A squid plays the trumpet, a crab taps the beat,
While dolphins jump in with their fancy skate feat.
The bubbles pop loud, laughter fills the sea,
As starfish applaud with a glee that's so free!

Enigmatic Radiance

A creature so bright, with a flick and a flash,
Wobbles on by, causing quite the clash.
'Tis a party, they say, in the deep of the night,
With glowing confetti that brings pure delight!

A fish in a top hat, what a quirky attire,
Juggles some pearls, setting hearts on fire.
All under the sea, laughter bubbles up high,
As creatures in colors take off to the sky!

A Sea of Lanterns

Beneath the waves, a festival springs,
With fish wearing hats and glittering rings.
They twinkle and shimmer, a dazzling sight,
As they dance in formation, oh, what a night!

An octopus chef spills spaghetti so bright,
He claims it's gourmet, but it's quite a fright.
With a wink and a nudge, the shrimp take a bite,
And giggles erupt in the moon's silver light!

Chronicles of Luminous Creatures

In tales of the sea, a tale so absurd,
A sea bass who thinks that he can sing a herd.
With lips that are flapping, and jokes to be shared,
He wobbles along, and he's slightly impaired!

A clownfish joins in, with a wink and a grin,
Shouting, "Come on, let's all join the spin!"
But the turtle just yawns, and takes a slow glide,
While the jellyfish dances with bubbles of pride!

Illuminated Whispers

In the deep where giggles grow,
A fish with a glow puts on a show.
With winks and blinks he beams his cheer,
Filling the dark with fishy jeer.

Sardines gather, rolling in mirth,
Laughing about his sparkling birth.
A disco ball in a watery ball,
His shining charm is a call to all.

Shimmering Shadows Below

In shadowy depths where the seaweed sways,
A lanternfish struts, brightening the bays.
He tickles clownfish, saying with glee,
"Look at my glow—can you see me?"

His buddies chuckle, a shimmering crew,
With each little dance, they light up the blue.
They argue and joke like pals in a race,
Beneath waves, they giggle and twirl in space.

Radiance in Dark Waters

Beneath the surface, a quirky sight,
A fish with a smile that's oh-so-bright.
He flashes his fins, creates a parade,
In the dark of the ocean, he's never afraid.

With bubbles of laughter that rise and pop,
He twirls and he whirls, and never will stop.
The seaweed joins in, swaying along,
All singing together a bubbly song.

Celestial Dances Beneath Waves

In the depths of night where the sea stars twinkle,
A lit-up fish makes the shadows crinkle.
With a jig and a reel, he rules the scene,
The underwater dance floor, so sleek and clean.

His friends all gather for a goofy spin,
With glimmers and glows, let the fun begin!
A splash and a dash, they twirl like a breeze,
Underwater parties that tickle with ease.

Glow of the Undersea Night

In the dark, where fish do prance,
A glow invites a silly dance.
With fins that flutter, tails that twist,
They wiggle and they flick their mist.

A crab in shades of neon hue,
Claims he's the star—oh who knew?
"Come join my party, don't be shy!
We'll have a blast 'neath the sea sky!"

A jellyfish with disco flair,
Swings to tunes in salty air.
"Dance, you fools, it's quite the show!
Just mind the anchor—don't say whoa!"

Fishes giggle, bubbles burst,
With every jig, they quench their thirst.
As laughter echoes through the tide,
Their aquatic joy, they can't hide.

Tales from the Fluorescent Depths

In the silence, shadows creep,
But watch out where the jellies leap!
They tell tales of wobbly fun,
And glow like crazies in the sun.

A squid recites his finest joke,
While bubbles bounce from fish who smoke.
"Why did the shrimp cross the floor?
To get to the other tide shore!"

Seahorses wear their glittered best,
Declaring they're the sea's true jest.
With pearl necklaces and silly hats,
They strut and prance, just like cool cats.

An octopus with eight left feet,
Tries to dance but can't find the beat.
The crowd erupts in joyous cheer,
"Just twist and twirl, there's naught to fear!"

Luminous Tales of the Abyss

In the cool of deep blue night,
Fish with sparkles bring delight.
They tell tales of ocean plight,
With laughter echoing, oh so bright!

A lobster pulls off a funky move,
While clams declare, "Let's get in groove!"
With wiggles and silly sweeps,
There's no time for tired heaps.

"Have you heard the gossip flow?
About the shark that's too slow?"
Giggling, they swim past the tide,
No friendly issues, just fishy pride.

The anemone joins in the fun,
Flashing colors like it's a gun.
"Don't forget to laugh today,
We'll dance beneath the salty spray!"

Underwater Reveries

In the depth where bright lights twinkle,
A dolphin's chuckle makes you crinkle.
"Let's start a battle, who's the best?
With flip and flop—we're on a quest!"

Clownfish hide with grins so wide,
Playing tricks where giggles abide.
"Why did the turtle wear a tie?
To look sharp, it's not a lie!"

Bubbles weave through coral gates,
Drawing us closer to their fates.
"Come join us! Don't miss the show,
Where silly antics freely flow!"

As currents twirl and fish collide,
Laughter rings as friends subside.
Together bright, together right,
We swim and sway through the night.

Radiance in Darkness

In the depths, where shadows creep,
A tiny bulb begins to peep.
It shakes its tail with joyful glee,
A disco party for fish, you see.

With big-eyed friends who twirl around,
They dance on waves, no sound, no bound.
Bubbles burst with tales so bright,
In this deep sea, they laugh at fright.

Glimmering Tales of the Ocean

A fish with flair, all lit up right,
Winks at crabs, oh what a sight!
'Tell me your secret!' a starfish pleads,
'Is it gel? Or just magic seeds?'

Undersea jokes that tickle fins,
With shimmering scales, the laughter spins.
They jest about who's the brightest star,
While sea cucumbers wonder just who they are.

Ethereal Flickers

Twinkling bulbs in swirling blue,
Who knew fish could be this true?
They hold a contest for best glow,
While a shy clam watches, 'Oh no!'

One fish trips, another slips,
But still they giggle through the zips.
With laughter echoing through the sea,
The deep can make you light and free.

Beneath the Surface Glow

In the dark, an eager grin,
A winking fish invites the din.
Spinning tales of treasure bright,
They toast with shells, what a delight!

The ocean's choir might sing low,
But their antics bring a charming show.
Flickering giggles in every wave,
For laughter is the light they crave.

Glow Beneath the Waves

In the deep where shadows play,
A fish with flair makes quite a display.
He wiggles and jiggles, oh what a sight,
With a flick of his tail, he glows in the night.

His friends swim close, they giggle and laugh,
Chasing the shimmer, a luminous gaffe.
Around the rocks, they frolic and glide,
A disco party, in the ocean so wide.

When a crab shows up, it thinks it's so sly,
But he trips on a barnacle, oh my, oh my!
With shrimps all around, they roast him with glee,
"Next time, dear crab, just let it be free!"

So under the waves, where the currents twist,
The glow of the sea brings a smile we can't miss.
Upon the ocean's floor, the laughter is found,
In the belly of the deep, joy forever unbound.

Illuminated Abyss

Down where the sunbeams refuse to go,
Lives a fish with a sparkle that steals the show.
His lantern-like charm lights up every scale,
With a grin that can make a whale turn pale.

Fishy friends gather, with bubbles to burst,
In the illuminated abyss, they never are cursed.
A seahorse jigs while the octopus moans,
"Is that glow from your belly or just your funny bones?"

The sand is soft—perfect for a dance,
They twirl and they swirl, take the chance!
A squid does a jig, with ink in the air,
Leaving everyone laughing, without a care.

In this underwater realm, where mischief thrives,
It's the glow that unites all the silly lives.
As the tides rise and fall, they share many a tale,
Of the fish with the glow who made laughter prevail.

Dance of Bioluminescence

In the glimmering depths, they wiggle and sway,
Flickering lights guide the fish on their way.
With a dance so electric, they glide through the blue,
Who knew that a fish could do the cha-cha too?

A pufferfish pouts, trying hard to impress,
While the group of bright minnows just can't help but bless.
They leap and they twirl, showing off their flair,
As anemones giggle, waving high in the air.

A grumpy old grouper looks in from his nook,
Wonders how these fish have such moves and suchooks.
"Back in my day, we just swam around,"
The critters all chuckle, what a silly sound!

So they dance and they prance in their unique style,
With a sparkle of joy that stretches for miles.
In this merry marine, where the glow shines bright,
They're the kings of the dance floor, the stars of the night.

Secrets of the Depths

In the ocean so deep, secrets are kept,
A fish with a wink, drives the others inept.
He whispers to crabs, "I've got tricks up my fin,
The funniest tales that will make you all grin!"

An anglerfish blushing, a light on his crown,
Feels silly and awkward, like he's wearing a gown.
But he joins in the fun, with a nod and a wink,
"Let's share our best jokes, till we all start to sink!"

So off they go, telling tales full of cheer,
Of bubble-blowing seahorses and a fish with no ear.
The laughter erupts like a bubbly sea foam,
In the heart of the ocean, they've found a new home.

With secrets now shared, bonds sparkling like light,
They've turned into legends, glowing bright with delight.
In the depths of the sea, amidst laughter and glee,
The fish tell their stories, wild and free!

Bioluminescent Dreams

In the ocean's cloak, they waddle and prance,
Little glowing guys in a fishy dance.
With a flick and a flash, they turn on the charm,
Making fishy friends feel safe and warm.

One thought they were stars, twinkling so bright,
But ended up jamming with a jellyfish tonight.
They sang underwater, a bubbly refrain,
Who knew the deep could host such a gain?

A squid tried to join with a whirl and a spin,
Only to find it was out of the fin.
With laughter that echoed through coral and foam,
They made the whole ocean feel like a home.

Glimmers in the Abyss

In the depths where it's dark and a little bit grim,
A flash of a grin from a fish with a whim.
They giggle and glow with a bubbly delight,
Playing hide and seek in the dark of the night.

"Catch me if you can!" the little fish cheered,
But the grumpy old grouper just sneered and heared.
"Why don't you hurry, you slippery sprite?
I'll turn off my gloom and join in your light!"

With a wink and a blink, the party began,
As an octopus joined with a salsa plan.
They danced in the deep, so silly and spry,
Who knew the abyss could throw such a high?

A lobster with glowsticks led them astray,
But who needs a map in this glowing ballet?
Together they twinkled, a luminous crew,
With glimmers in the depths, they made quite a stew.

Echoes of the Deep

In a watery world where the giggles abound,
Echoes of laughter roll all around.
A trumpetfish trumpets, a rascal's delight,
While a flatfish plays peekaboo out of sight.

They dive and they dash, with a splashy loud cheer,
Making bubbles that pop and then vanish sheer.
Octopi juggle while turtles do flips,
Oh, the magic of underwater quips!

Seahorses trot with a wobble and sway,
Telling tales of adventures from yesterday.
With whispers and giggles that ripple and flow,
They keep the deep laughing, giving fish quite a show.

Neon Secrets of the Sea

Beneath the blue waves where the secrets abound,
Neon fish sparkle, in pranks they are crowned.
A clownfish is giggling, doing pretend,
While pufferfish puff and say, "You're my friend!"

Swirls of bright colors, they flutter and flash,
Creating a carnival with a whimsical splash.
Anglerfish chuckles, "You'll never believe,
I caught a good joke up my sleeve!"

With glow-in-the-dark parties on coral they hold,
They tell silly stories, both new and old.
In a world down below, full of humor and glee,
Who knew such fun lurked beneath the deep sea?

Silent Beacons of the Deep Blue

In the ocean's dark embrace,
Dance the fish with silly grace,
Flashing smiles, a glowing flair,
Who knew fish could comb their hair?

With every flick, a joke they share,
Wiggling tails, what a pair!
Dancing shadows, oh so bright,
They giggle in the depth of night.

Bubbles bubble, laughter's near,
Who knew fish could drink a beer?
With lanterns lit, they hold a feast,
Making friends, to say the least.

In this realm, no need for dread,
Just fishy tales, all widespread!
As they twirl in hues so bold,
The deep blue giggles, purest gold.

Symphony of Glowing Abyss

In a symphony of glimmer bright,
Fish skate and twirl, what a sight!
They sing of seas and laugh so loud,
Dressing up, they're quite the crowd!

A jokester fish, with dots like fries,
Cracking jokes as the sea flies,
With each flash, a tale unfolds,
Of undersea antics, oh so bold!

The crab plays drums, a merry beat,
While seahorses tap their feet,
They float and spin, what a thrill,
Catch a fish for dinner? Never will!

An opera of bubbles fills the air,
They giggle in bubbles, without a care,
Underneath waves, the tales are spun,
In the glowing depths, they all have fun.

Flickering Souls Beneath the Waves

Flickering spirits dance and sway,
In quirky forms, they love to play,
With a wink and a glow, they tease,
Laughing lightly with the breeze.

Beneath the waves, they hide and seek,
In colors bright and shades unique,
Fish in costumes, what a crime,
All for laughs, they waste no time!

A shimmering star, with a goofy grin,
Makes seaweed hats for the kin,
All around, the sea creatures cheer,
As they sway their lanterns near.

Join the dance, let worries cease,
For in these depths, there's only peace,
Beneath the waves, they glimmer and shine,
Flickering souls, laughter divine.

Ethereal Glow in Ink Black

In ink-black seas, the fun begins,
With glowing friends who wear big grins,
They flip and flop, burst with delight,
In a parade of colors, shining bright!

Disco fish sporting funky shoes,
Grooving together, they never lose,
While ghostly squids wave with flair,
They twirl around without a care.

The deep is a stage, the stars their lights,
Where jellyfish dance on magic nights,
They crack jokes with glowing glee,
As the ocean tunes to their silly spree.

So come, dive deep into this laugh,
Join the play, take a photograph,
For in this glow, in swirling ambers,
Laughter lives in Undersea Jamborees!

Phosphorescent Dreams

In waters deep where shadows play,
The fish chuckle in their glow,
Tiny lanterns on a display,
Dancing disco, oh what a show!

They wiggle and they giggle bright,
While bubbles burst like fireworks,
Each flash a beacon, pure delight,
In this undersea, silly network!

Their smiles shine with every peek,
Like underwater jesters at their game,
In phosphorescent hues they sneak,
Chasing darkness, it's never the same!

So join the party, take a dive,
With luminous friends who love to tease,
In their ocean of laughter, we thrive,
Under the waves where joy's a breeze!

The Essence of Aquatic Light

Beneath the waves, a curious sight,
The fish have hats made of shine,
Each glimmer a giggle, oh what a fright,
In their brilliant underwater line!

With blinks and winks, they make their case,
A comedy club beneath the sea,
Where every flicker has a face,
And laughter flows like a bubbly spree!

They hold a contest, who can glow best,
With silly stunts and funny moves,
The brightest one wins a shiny jest,
In this aquatic dance that grooves!

So dive in deep, don't miss the fun,
Join our finned friends in their bright parade,
Where the essence of giggles has just begun,
In the light of the ocean, we're never afraid!

Fluid Rhythms of the Deep

A wiggly dance down in the blue,
Where fish with lights create a scene,
They shimmy and shake in every hue,
In their radiant underwater routine!

Each flicker a cue to bob and weave,
With every glow, they start to cheer,
In the fluid rhythm, don't take leave,
Join in the fun, there's nothing to fear!

A school of laughter swims through the tide,
With gills that giggle and tails that sway,
They put on shows, no need to hide,
In the wavy world of joy, let's play!

So let's twirl and whirl in this grand ballet,
Where joy becomes a bubbly escape,
In the depths, where seafolk come out to play,
In the splash of light, we take shape!

A Flicker Away from Darkness

In the dark deep blue, a spark ignites,
Fish wearing smiles, quite the affair,
Their laughter is the joy of nights,
With bands of brightness everywhere!

They twirl around, a glowing twist,
Like colorful lights on a festival night,
With every flash, a bubble missed,
These merry fish are such a sight!

Each flicker, a jest they make,
With silly antics, they swim and tease,
In this watery world, fun's at stake,
Where blinking friends sway with ease!

So wade on in and join the fun,
A flicker away from gloom and dread,
In the ocean's heart, we all be one,
Where laughter bubbles and colors spread!

The Deep's Dazzling Canvas

In the depths where critters play,
A fish with sparkles goes its way.
It wiggles, it giggles, in the glow,
Painting the ocean with a funny show.

With fins that dance, a silly twist,
A friend to all, how could you resist?
An artist of bubbles, it swirls with glee,
Making the deep a sight to see.

Who needs a brush when you've got a tail?
Inking the waves with a bubbly trail.
This underwater circus brings such cheer,
Where laughter bubbles, and joy is near.

So next time you dive, just take a glance,
At the flashy fish who loves to prance.
In the vibrant blue, it leads the way,
Turning the ocean to a bright ballet.

Marine Choreography

Under the waves, a dance ignites,
Weird fish flutter in sparkling lights.
Not one follows the same old beat,
They shimmy and shake with flippered feet.

A creature glides with a shiny grin,
Who knew the ocean could have such spin?
It bumps and bounces, no care in the world,
While all of its sparkles are swirled and twirled.

The clams clap shells like they're in a band,
While the seaweed sways, oh so grand!
Anemones sway, they join the flair,
Every wave a burst of silly air.

So come join the fun under watery beams,
Where fish do tricks that defy all dreams.
In this aqua stage, no one feels blue,
Just a parade of giggles, and lots of woo-hoo!

Drawn to the Glimmer

A flicker, a flash, what's that I see?
A fish with sparkles, come look at me!
It flits through the coral, a dazzling sight,
Turning the ocean into pure delight.

With each little twirl, it winks with flair,
Creating ripples of joyous air.
They giggle and wiggle, in quirky ways,
A splash of fun that brightens the days.

Bubbles are popping, laughter's afloat,
As fish gather 'round in a happy boat.
They trade funny stories, and giggle some more,
In the shimmering shadows, they're never a bore.

So if you're feeling blue and down,
Just peek at the sea, where smiles abound.
For in these deep waters, you will discover,
A world full of charm, like none another!

Celestial Echoes in the Sea

Amid the dark where the shadows creep,
Danced creatures shimmer in laughter's leap.
A glow in the abyss, a radiant cheer,
Makes all the fish feel less of fear.

They twirl and whirl in a galactic spread,
A wiggling party, not a one of them dread.
Tentacles flailing as they beam with glee,
Singing the tunes of the sparkling sea.

With each glowing flick, they send out a jest,
Who knew the ocean could be such a fest?
In this underwater rave, all are pals,
Creating a wonderland, giggles, and gaffs.

So whenever you feel lost or blue,
Remember this paradise, welcoming you.
Where laughter echoes in bubbles and beams,
In the depths of the sea, joy reigns in dreams.

Whispers Among Tidal Currents

In the depths where shadows play,
Fish gossip about their day.
Sardines swirl with tales so sly,
While octopuses wink an eye.

Jellyfish float, their dance so neat,
Ballet of currents, oh what a treat!
Seahorses prance in their grand parade,
Flipping and flopping, in colors displayed.

Crabs click in a comedic song,
Telling tales of where they belong.
Laughter bubbles from gurgling brine,
As sand castles form in a line.

Anemones wave with floppy arms,
Inviting fish to share their charms.
Giggles ripple through coral streets,
A party hosted by fishy feats.

Vitae of the Echoing Deep

In a kingdom where blubbering reigns,
Whales sing of their silly gains.
Deep-sea creatures with pearly smiles,
Share laughter that stretches for miles.

Starfish play tic-tac-toe on rocks,
Mollusks wear shells like fancy socks.
Every gurgle, a comedic twist,
In a vast ocean, none can resist.

A shrimp recites a joke so punny,
While dolphins can't stop, it's just too funny.
Giant squids, in their inky bloom,
Draw doodles like kids in the gloom.

With bubbles rising, the humor grows,
As the nautilus strikes a silly pose.
Life in the depths, a wacky dance,
Where every creature takes a chance.

Chasing Glimmers

Glimmers flutter near and far,
Fish darting like a racing car.
Tiny lights in a swirling sea,
Leading friends on a quest with glee.

A pufferfish wonders, 'What's the show?'
While gobies wiggle, stealing the glow.
They chase the sparkle, a merry band,
Splashing 'round the seaweed strand.

Lanterns flicker on kelp forests,
As they tease like playful jesters.
The silliness carries near the shore,
As fish giggle and swim some more.

With each pulse, the water sings,
"Let's dance a jig, let's spread our wings!"
In this treasure hunt of laughter found,
Joy bubbles forth, a priceless sound.

A World of Dappled Radiance

In a world where colors gleam,
Amidst the waves, the fish all beam.
Clownfish giggle, a welcome sight,
As they swim in the dappled light.

Sea turtles shuffle with graceful flair,
In a sea party, none could compare.
They share stories of great delight,
Even the barnacles join the sight.

With every flick of a fin, they sway,
Making shadows dance, they love to play.
A group of fish forms a conga line,
Twisting and rolling, it's simply divine.

As sea cucumbers chuckle with grace,
All join in for a frolicsome race.
In this underwater carnival bright,
Everyone is a star in the festive light.

Beaconing Dreams

In the depths where shadows play,
A fish flickers, bright as day.
With a wink and a silly grin,
It leads the way, let the games begin!

Swirling around in a goofy dance,
Its glow pulls others in a trance.
Every flick shines with delight,
Making bubbles that tickle the night.

A grumpy crab shakes his claw,
Fumbling around without a flaw.
But the fish just laughs and glows,
Brightening up the thorniest woes.

Through tangled seaweed, they whirl and twirl,
Creating chaos, what a swirl!
With giggles echoing in the deep,
It's a party where no one sleeps!

The Enchantment of Deep Waters

In waters where gunk and grit reside,
A fish with a glow takes joy in the ride.
With each bubbly joke that it throws,
The murky depths laugh from head to toes.

A crusty old eel rolls its eyes in disdain,
But the lantern glow won't be tamed by the mundane.
It zips and zags through coral caverns,
Announcing a party of the wackiest manner!

Octopuses join in, waving their arms,
Caught in the magic, charmed by the charms.
No seaweed's too tangled, no fish too shy,
When the glowboat starts sailing, spirits fly high!

So here's to the fish, the jester of tides,
With a humor that tickles, wherever it glides.
Through the gloomiest trenches, their giggles resound,
In the enchantment of waters, joy knows no bounds!

Glows of a Midnight Sea

In the midnight sea where laughter's a theme,
A fish glows bright, like a water-based dream.
With a flick of its tail and a jolly dance,
It sends the night critters into a trance.

"Follow me, friends!" it bubbles with glee,
As creatures come wiggling from every degree.
From sea stars to snails, the parade's quite a sight,
As they shimmy and cheese in the shimmering light.

A clam shuts tight with a cheery "oh no!",
While dolphins leap high, putting on quite a show.
The jellyfish glow like lanterns afloat,
Bringing giggles and joy, as they slide on a boat!

In this underwater rave, nothing goes wrong,
The rhythm of bubbles becomes a sweet song.
So here's to the fish with its jovial beam,
In the midnight sea, we're all part of the dream!

Fish that Dance with Stars

Beneath the waves where the universe twirls,
A fish prances, making the whole ocean swirl.
Its glow twinkles brighter than stars in the sky,
In a grand cosmic fest, giving laughter a try.

The starfish roll over, trying to spin,
While the giggling angler fish joins in the din.
With each silly jig, the critters unite,
In a dance that ignites the dazzling night.

"Catch me if you can!" the fish shouts with glee,
As bubbles burst forth in a shimmering spree.
It weaves through the eels, twirls 'round a sprout,
Crashing into a rock, while the crowd lets out a shout!

And as the show ends, they bow with flair,
The sea is aglow, and joy fills the air.
In the depths of the ocean, under stars so bright,
They found a rhythm that made everything right!

Celestial Lights Beneath

In the deep where fish play hide and seek,
A glowing fry with a sparkly cheek.
He jokes all day in his sea-silk suit,
Chasing bubbles and a ticklish spook.

With every flash, he tells a pun,
To all the crabs who run for fun.
"Why do fish never get lost?
They follow the currents, that's the cost!"

With friends like shrimp and silly eels,
They gather for a rousing meal.
"Don't eat the glow-worm, it's my pet!
He glimmers more than the best sunset!"

As waves dance along the ocean's floor,
Giggles bubble and laughter galore.
Each flicker brightens the midnight scene,
Where fish turn jokes into a playful sheen.

Chronicles of the Night Sea

Under waves where shadows fall,
Live fish who can't resist a brawl.
With a wink and a glow, they take the stage,
Performing antics, the ocean's rage.

A squid with ink plays prankster hard,
As others gather, cheeks all scarred.
"What's the secret to your nimble dance?
Just wiggle your fins and take a chance!"

Between the rocks, they tell tall tales,
Of daring escapes from slippery snails.
"Why swim so fast? It's quite a theme,
I'm late for last night's fishing dream!"

As creatures glow with laughter's grace,
They twirl and leap in the vast embrace.
The ocean's deep, a comedy show,
With echoes of giggles in each undertow!

Neon Ripples

In waters where the glowfish meet,
A shimmering dance on slippery feet.
They share their jokes in colored beams,
While puffers laugh in bubble screams.

"Why was the starfish so good at math?
He counted the tides, took every path!"
With tails a-swish, they spin and twirl,
Across the sea like a merry whirl.

A lantern tooth with a crooked grin,
Sings silly songs from the bay's deep skin.
"I've got a light that shines so bright,
I'll guide you home without a fright!"

In the depths where laughter swims,
Whimsical tales are never dimmed.
With glowing friends, the night is fun,
As neon ripples spark and run!

Tides of Radiant Mysteries

Beneath the waves, where secrets dwell,
A fishy farce, oh what a swell!
With each bright flicker, they share a jest,
In a world where laughter is the best.

"Why don't sharks like to play charades?
They can't keep a secret; it just invades!"
With giggles rising from ocean beds,
Mysteries unfold in bouncing threads.

A prancing dolphin shimmies near,
Telling tales that bring good cheer.
"Why does the ocean never get cold?
It has all the fish-blood stories told!"

As tides roll in, they dance and spin,
In moonlit waters, cheeky grins.
Radiant frolics amid the bliss,
In currents of laughter, they can't miss!

A Dance of Light in the Darkness

In the depths where shadows play,
Little fish with glow display.
They wiggle, they jiggle, what a sight,
Dancing around in the ocean's night.

With goofy grins and fins that sway,
These glowing sprites start their ballet.
Flippers flap and bubbles burst,
Making every fish feel immersed.

A party bright beneath the waves,
They tease the crabs, the little knaves.
In the gloom, their lights beam so merry,
Who knew deep seas could be so cheery?

They twirl and spin, a shimmered spree,
It's a disco ball for a wiggly spree.
So grab a partner, don't you frown,
Let's boogie down where it's never brown!

Bioluminescent Serenade

In the blue where silence reigns,
Fish on a mission, no strain on their brains.
They flicker bright with a humorous plea,
'Come join our swim, just take a 'glee'!

With jokes in bubbles, they flutter and glide,
Crabs try to join but find they can't hide.
'What is this glow—are we in a jam?'
'The coolest rave—now don't be a clam!'

The glow is a song, a melody bright,
A swirling performance that just feels right.
Fish chomping seaweed, making a mess,
Grooving around, oh what happiness!

They serenade the moon with a laugh,
Sharing their glow like a photograph.
So if you dive down into this show,
Expect a giggle in each little glow!

Secrets of the Aquatic Glow

Down below where no one see,
Lives a school of luminous glee.
They whisper secrets, share their light,
'Just don't let the sharks in on our delight!'

With silly grins and winks of bright,
Swerving past fishes in sheer delight.
'Who needs a lantern? We have our flair!'
Brightly shining without a care.

They gather in circles, a glowing bond,
Telling tales of the beyond.
'Oh, did you hear about the anglerfish's trick?'
'Ha! Bet he wishes he was glowingly slick!'

In this quirky world beneath the sea,
Humor flows just like the spree.
So if you swim through shadows and tides,
Expect to chuckle where laughter resides!

Flickering Dreams in the Deep

In the ocean's belly, dreams take a flight,
Little fishie winks with sheer delight.
'Why swim alone when we can glow?
Let's light up the night with our little show!'

They glide in patterns, all shapes and sizes,
Winking at predators, oh what surprises!
'Catch us if you can, you slippery sneak!'
Their lights turn off when the fish start to freak.

In a slapstick routine, dimples appear,
With glow-in-the-dark charms bringing cheer.
They beam with laughter, such playful rays,
Chasing each other in flashing displays.

Flickers and sparkles; the current's sweet,
An underwater circus with an upbeat beat.
When the tides say goodbye, it's a blink and a tease,
They disappear into twilight with giggles and glees!

Mysteries of the Marine Twilight

In darkness waves take flight,
Glowing wonders dance with delight.
Fish with bulbs, in a silly spree,
Who needs a lamp? Just look at me!

Bubbles pop like tiny glee,
Bioluminescent, what a sight to see!
Flashy tails twirl in the night,
An underwater party, oh what a plight!

Crown jewels drift with laughter near,
With tiny glowworms singing cheer.
In this playful gleam, all converge,
A comedy sketch, as shadows surge!

So dive into this giggling sea,
Where jumpy jellies sway so free.
Aquatic chuckles echo so bright,
In the whimsical depths of the night!

Guiding Beacons of the Deep

Beyond the surf, oh what a show,
A flickering wink from the depths below.
Fishes with flashlights, what a sight,
Fishy fools chasing their own light!

Flashing every hue, they twirl and dive,
In this brightly lit, quirk-filled hive.
Each spark ignites a hearty laugh,
As creatures of the sea dance their path.

Anglerfish grinning, tuggin' your cap,
"Join the fun!" he says with a flap.
Beacons of giggles in the blue,
Where laughter bubbles up anew!

So come take a peek in this glowing domain,
With silly sea critters, what's there to gain?
Just a night of chuckles and playful fades,
In the guiding glow of the ocean's charades!

Luminous Whispers

Whispers of color beneath the sea,
Jellyfish giggle, "Look at me!"
With tentacles wiggling, oh so fine,
These glowing pals are having a time!

A wink from a shrimp, oh isn't it neat,
In the disco of fish, there's quite a beat!
Dancing bubbles taking a chance,
In this glowing sashay, there's a fishy dance.

Glowsticks abound in this aquatic night,
Whispers of giggles, a marine delight.
Every shimmer tells a funny tale,
As waves and creatures set their sails.

So swim with a grin 'neath the starlit spark,
Where the sea comes alive with a bubbling lark.
In luminous laughter, the night unfolds,
With stories of joy in the ocean retold!

Sparking Dreams in the Sea

In the deep, where the oddballs roam,
Fishes glow bright, call it their home.
With a flash and a flick, they merrily play,
Dreaming in colors, come join the ballet!

Starry-eyed squids with a glow to share,
Twinkling like stars in the midnight air.
They'll joke and jest in a wavy mess,
In dreams of the deep, who needs to impress?

Anemones chuckling, "Aren't we grand?"
Pulling pranks with a colorful hand.
Each glimmer ignites giggles galore,
As sea life sparkles, who could ask for more?

So delve into waters where humor gleams,
In the ocean's embrace, find your dreams.
With every sparkle, let laughter flow,
Adventure awaits, let the fun overflow!

Guides of the Midnight Tide

In depths so dark, the fish do glow,
They navigate where few dare go.
With silly grins, they lead the way,
While grumpy crabs just yell, "No way!"

Flashing smiles in the ocean's chill,
Chasing shrimp with relentless skill.
A party starts beneath the waves,
Where seaweed dances, all misbehaves!

Caught in a whirl of sparkling cheer,
The fish throw bubbles, loud and clear.
An undersea rave, it's quite absurd,
Where even the shyest dolphins stir!

So here's to the farcical fish parade,
A jolly crew in sea's charade.
With flicks and flares, they twirl and glide,
Those jesters of the moody tide!

Vestiges of Fluorescent Nights

In the dark, their colors flare,
Like disco balls, restoring flair.
They wiggle through the muck and mire,
Creating laughs that swim like fire!

The starfish clap with giddy force,
While angler fish plot a funny course.
A party down in the briny deep,
Where even the octopus can't help but leap!

Old crab complains, 'Who turned the lights?'
But join the fun, ignore the frights.
For every flash is a groovy beat,
Even sharks can't resist their fancy feet!

So when the night wraps its blackened hue,
Just look for the glow with a smile askew.
In the ocean's quest for jest and cheer,
You'll find the fish dancing without fear!

Light-Bearers of the Sea Floor

On the sandy floor where the silly play,
The sparkling blinks make night like day.
With fins that flutter, and tails that spin,
They laugh at the fish who can't quite win!

The clams all giggle, the lobsters prance,
In this absurd fluorescence dance.
Even the sea cucumbers roll and jive,
If only our world could come alive!

The bubbles rise like tunes from a chart,
While groupers flash their brightened art.
A shimmery world in the ocean chest,
Where humor adds to the fishy fest!

With winks and blinks in a swirl of fun,
They light the sea till the night is done.
For these jesting fish, they've got it right,
Bringing joy to every wondrous night!

Echoes of Luminous Pasts

The memories glow like a playful spark,
As fish tell tales in the frothy dark.
With flicking fins and twinkling eyes,
They share their legends beneath ocean skies.

Glowing whispers of what once was,
Squeaky laughs without a pause.
In bubbling waters, they stitch the tale,
Of how the sea threw shades of pale!

From the depths where the lore runs deep,
These giggling fish refuse to sleep.
For even when the night gets sore,
Their antics echo, forever more!

With every shimmery tale they weave,
They lighten hearts and make us believe.
For life's a dance in the ocean swirl,
With every laugh, the waves unfurl!

Flickers of Forgotten Tales

In the depths where bubbles sing,
A fish with sparkles does its thing.
It giggles bright, a silly sight,
As shadows dance and lose their fright.

With a flick and flap, it tells a joke,
To grumpy crabs, it hopes to poke.
They chuckle loud, they can't resist,
As bubbles burst with a splashy twist.

Each tale spun beneath the sea,
Turns frowns to grins, oh joy, oh glee.
This fishy jester swims with pride,
Leaving all the gloom outside.

From the floor, the tales take flight,
Where laughter echoes, dark turns bright.
Though tales may fade like sea foam's trail,
The fun is real, it cannot fail.

Woven Light Below

In the dark where the seaweed grows,
A fishy giggle, a ticklish nose.
It weaves a glow with twisted glee,
While friends swim near, they laugh with glee.

Oh what a sight, a dazzling flash,
As jellybeans in a jelly clash.
Tiny twinklers join the fun,
When nighttime falls, their games begun.

They play hide and seek in coral's maze,
While sea slugs smile in funny ways.
With bubbles blown and laughter loud,
This sparkling troupe makes shadows proud.

It's a party where all are bright,
Dressed in gleams and a wink of light.
For no one can frown or sigh,
With such a crew as they drift by.

An Ocean's Odyssey

A fish in quest of joy and fun,
Goes on adventures, oh what a run!
It rolls with sea stars, quite absurd,
And tells tall tales without a word.

With a wink and flick of its tail so grand,
It finds a treasure buried in sand.
A shiny thing, a bucket or two,
Which truly makes the ocean blue.

Clams applaud with a raucous cheer,
As squids dance near, tossing their gear.
They all dive down, sea shenanigans reign,
In this underwater comedy train.

So off they swim, this merry bunch,
With giggles shared over dinner lunch.
The ocean's secrets, so wild and free,
Are best explored with laughter's decree.

The Hidden Glow

In a crevice, something glows,
It's not a pearl, it's quite the show!
A comedy club for fishy guests,
With jokes and jests, who needs the rest?

A grinning shark is the star of the night,
Telling tales that give all a fright.
But wink, wink, hoot, it's all in fun,
As everyone triggers a splashy pun.

Anglerfish sports a curvy grin,
Inviting all, come gather in!
The spotlight's glow is just for laughs,
As octopuses pull silly gaffes.

So dive into trashy, giddy delight,
Where laughter bubbles up bright with might.
Under the waves where the giggles flow,
There's magic found in a slip and a glow.

Beneath the Surface: A Luminous Tale

In the deep, where shadows loom,
A fish with a glow makes the dark a zoom.
With a flick of its tail, it causes a scene,
Dancing like a star in the ocean's green.

It teases the crabs with a wiggly flash,
While turtles giggle and dance in a splash.
The seahorses chuckle at the sight so bright,
As fish play hide-and-seek in the night.

"Catch me if you can!" the fish starts to boast,
To the sleepy old shrimp who missed out on toast.
With glowing whispers, they play all around,
In a shimmering waltz without making a sound.

But who needs a lamp when your scale's like a gem?
Said the quirky fish, "I'm a birthday for them!"
So beneath the waves, where the giggles flare,
Laughter and glimmers fill the salty air.

Radiant Trails in the Ocean's Vein

A fish zooms past with a twinkle on show,
Leaving trails like sparklers, a watery glow.
The snails roll their eyes, 'What a silly sight!'
As bubbles erupt in a laugh-out-loud flight.

The octopus grins, with his ink-pots in tow,
Planning to join in the luminous flow.
He paints all the corals in colors so grand,
Turning the reef into a glow-in-the-hand.

With shimmery friends at the sea's lively ball,
They whirl and they spin, what a bright free-for-all!
Even the oysters forget their own shells,
As they wiggle and giggle and share silly yells.

From deep down below to the surf up above,
A carnival of colors shining with love.
In laughter and light, they create a parade,
With each splash and shimmer, all worries fade.

Phosphorescent Storytellers

In the depths, where stories unfold,
Fish gather 'round, their scales a bright gold.
Each tale they tell dances in the dark,
With glowing punchlines that always hit the mark.

On a jellyfish stage, they perform with flair,
Witty as seaweed, they fill the salt air.
The flatfish tells tales of being quite flat,
While the pufferfish pops up, making all laugh at that!

A lanternfish boasts, "I can outshine the sun!"
While the clowns in the crowd snicker and run.
With glimmers and giggles, they brighten the night,
For each fish's humor is pure delight.

So gather, dear friends, for a show of great fun,
Where laughter and light chase the dark on the run.
In a world of sea critters, both clever and spry,
Their shimmering stories rise and glide by.

Glow of the Hidden Realm

Deep in the ocean where secrets get told,
A realm full of giggles, where fish are bold.
With lights like lanterns, they bounce here and there,
Creating a disco beneath the sea's care.

"Let's party!" yells one with a flickering grin,
As shrimp and small crabs scurry in to join in.
They boogie with currents and sway to the beat,
With jellyfish lights glowing bright at their feet.

The dolphin in costume shows off with a spin,
With sparkly sequins, what a fabulous win!
While the otters roll over in laughter and cheer,
For the ocean's a stage, as they dance without fear.

As bubbles are blown and adventures ignite,
The hidden realm sparkles with sheer delight.
In this wacky world, with a glow so divine,
Every creature's a star, in this water-wrapped time.

Secrets of the Ocean's Glow

In the deep where fish do play,
Glowing bright in a silly way,
Jellybean-shaped with a grin,
They dance around like they might win.

With flickers sharp as a wink,
They form a glow that makes you think,
Are they laughing beneath the tide?
Or are they just in a fishy ride?

Their beams are bright, their hearts are bold,
Telling tales that never get old,
"Hey! Over here! Come join the fun!"
In the ocean, we all run!

With bubbles popping, they make a shush,
While glow-worms sing and fish all hush,
In this playful, watery spot,
The hilarity can't be caught!

Twilight Traces in the Depths

In twilight hues where fishes dream,
They giggle softly, or so it seems,
With ticklish fins and goofy grins,
They're the jesters of the ocean's whims.

With trails of light that zig and zag,
They play hide and seek like a brag,
"Found you!" they chirp with a flash of flair,
Dancing through currents without a care.

In the depths, there's a party going strong,
As jellyfish whirl to a bubbly song,
With a wink and a swish, they spread their cheer,
Twilight traces that bring us near!

So come join in this frolicking jam,
With fish that giggle and playful clams,
In the sparkling sea, they twinkle all night,
Creating a door to giggles so bright!

Lanterns of the Midnight Current

When the moon takes a dip in the tide,
Little fish gather, they can't abide,
With lanterns bright, they light the sea,
In a flash of fun, they're wild and free.

Bouncing around like they own the show,
With sparkles and giggles all aglow,
"Catch me if you can!" they tease and flaunt,
Midnight jesters who dance and taunt.

Their lights swing low, their antics high,
As currents twirl, they just can't lie,
With a puff of bubbles, they leap and play,
Under the blanket of a starry sway.

Through midnight's charms, their laughter rings,
These lanterns shine with the joy they bring,
In a watery world where mirth doesn't end,
Each shimmering flash is a playful friend!

Luminous Travelers of the Depths

Travelers bright in the ocean's embrace,
With luminous trails and a bubbly face,
They ride the waves like they're in a race,
Every twist and turn brings a smile to trace.

In schools of giggles, they wander wide,
Winking at waves with a giggling glide,
"Did you see that? A shrimp just fell!"
Their laughter bubbles like a clam shell bell.

Crafting lanterns from jelly and light,
They paint the deep with colors so bright,
In a comical world where they play and frown,
For joy in the ocean will never drown.

So dance with us in this glimmering sphere,
With travelers bright, there's nothing to fear,
In the depths of the sea, we laugh and shout,
For silliness in the waves is what it's about!

Captured in Glimmers

In the deep, where big fish swim,
A tiny glow starts to brim.
A dance of spark, a flicker bright,
They giggle in their underwater light.

With silly grins and twinkling eyes,
They hide from predators, oh what a surprise!
They twirl and play, creating a show,
Low-key stars in the ocean's flow.

A glowstick party beneath the waves,
Knocking on shells, being quite brave.
Freestyle swimming, going in loops,
These little lanterns in colorful groups.

With fins like wands and a playful sway,
They brighten the night in their own quirky way.
Who knew the deep could be such fun?
With giggles and glee, their party's begun!

Luminous Threads of the Ocean

In waters deep, a yarn entwined,
With glowing threads of a kind!
A tapestry of giggles spun,
In the currents, watch them run!

A patchwork party, oh what a sight,
With flutters and flickers, pure delight.
They're weaving dreams, one glow at a time,
Underwater humor, a real-life rhyme!

Little fish showing off their flair,
Playing tag without a care.
A bubble burst, a splash, a gleam,
Creating a sparkle in every dream.

With colorful light in a grand parade,
These tiny jesters dance unafraid.
What a show as they frolic around,
Their ocean stage, where fun is found!

Beyond the Veil of Darkness

In the shadows where few dare tread,
A giggle erupts, surprise ahead!
With winks and shines that trip the night,
They make even darkness feel so light.

The stealthy jokes beneath the waves,
Riddles wrapped up in luminous caves.
They dart and dive with much-to-do,
Turning fear to fun with a playful 'Boo!'

A chorus of chuckles mixed with the tide,
With every flicker, their joy is wide.
Sneaking up where the seaweed sways,
They joke about their best hiding ways!

Wrap your heart in laughs so light,
For shadows here are filled with bright.
In the depths below, where musings play,
The little glow-fish snicker away!

Essence of Neon Shadows

In the neon glow of surprise and fun,
They dance like stars, everyone's number one!
With sparkly whispers and shimmering tails,
Joking about fins and their colorful scales.

A comedy show with upturned fins,
Making the ocean giggle with grins.
They flip and twist without a care,
These little jesters, bright and rare!

With jokes about shells and silly crabs,
They turn seaweed into fun jabs.
Each glimmer bursts with laughter's thrill,
Writing tales of joy, they always will!

In their colorful world, magical and bright,
Life is a joke and a dance in the night.
These little lights, a giggly spree,
In the ocean's laughter, we all agree!

Dancers of the Abyss

In the depths, they sway and sway,
With wiggly moves, they steal the play.
Fins like ribbons, they twirl in haste,
Who knew fish could dance with such taste?

Their disco balls are glowing bright,
Britches of coral, what a sight!
With a flick of the tail, and a sparkle or two,
They're the groovy kings of the ocean crew!

They invite the crabs to join the fun,
Underwater shindigs never just one!
Anemones giggle, sea cucumbers cheer,
What a krazy party, come and draw near!

So if you visit below the sea,
Buckle up, hold tight, we're livin' free!
The dancers of the abyss, oh what a scene,
With a splash and a laugh, it's a underwater dream!

Silhouettes of Aqua Light

In the shallows where shadows swirl,
Fishes prance in a watery whirl.
With glimmering scales and tales untold,
They play hide and seek, so brave and bold!

With bubbles and giggles, they all convene,
Flickering flashes, a flamboyant scene.
Here's a barracuda in a funky duet,
While seaweed twirls, you can't quite forget!

Silhouettes dance in a shimmering glow,
Swapping secrets that only they know.
"Wait for the drop!" shouts a playful catfish,
As they dive in a twist—it's their greatest wish!

Through rippling waters, they scatter and gleam,
Join in their frolic, it's quite the dream!
A show of light, laughter and fun,
Beneath the waves, the joy's never done!

Secrets in Shimmering Waters

In waters deep, where wonders bloom,
Swim secrets hidden in ocean's room.
Giggling shrimps tell tales so sly,
Beneath soft ripples, they just can't lie!

A jellyfish winks, with fluorescent flair,
As schools of guppies swirl in midair.
"Did you hear?", a seahorse whispers low,
About the crabs who throw a rave show!

The octopus grins, ink splashes like paint,
Sketching giggles, oh what a quaint!
"Join us now, it's the next big spree!"
Underwater chums, as fun as can be!

In shimmering waters where laughter is king,
Every dive is a joke, hear the bubbles sing!
Secrets shared, a bubbly toast,
To the fishy friends we love the most!

Ghosts of the Ocean Glow

In the midnight depths where shadows creep,
Ghostly fish with secrets to keep.
Waltzing through kelp, they share a grin,
Each flicker of fin, a bubbly spin!

With glowing bodies and a twinkle in sight,
They dance like phantoms in the moonlight.
Octopus moonwalks with such bliss,
Creating bubbles with every twist!

A parade of lights, a hilarious view,
Like a spooky show, but with a funny crew.
With a wink and a wave, they invite you in,
For a laughter-filled ride that won't ever thin!

So join these spirits and laugh with glee,
The ghosts of the ocean, wild and free.
Where jokes bubble up and spirits ignite,
In the underwater glow, life's a delight!

Underwater Starlight Odyssey

In the depths, where giggles swim,
Fish wear hats and sing a hymn.
Bubbles rise like laughing clowns,
Their bright glows turn frowns upside down.

Tiny lights dance in the swell,
Telling tales that no one can spell.
With every flicker, mischief unfolds,
Nautical secrets that never get old.

South of the sea, they throw a ball,
With jellyfish guests who trip and fall.
A party under waves so bright,
Where every fish is a beacon of light.

Swirls of bright colors, playful and bold,
In this wonderland, giggles take hold.
A lantern's wink, a gleeful cheer,
Join the fun, the ocean's festival here!

Veiled Radiance of the Ocean Floor

Masked fish wear shades, oh what a sight,
In swirls of liquid, dancing in light.
They twirl and twist like a goofy show,
Glow-worms cheer and put on a glow.

Crabs in tuxedos tapping their claws,
As they groove down below with fins and jaws.
The sand's not gray, but a lively hue,
When the ocean floor's a bustling zoo.

Jellyfish join, floating like balloons,
Singing oceanic, jazzy tunes.
With glowing smiles, the fish invite,
To join their wacky, warm delight.

Electric eels provide the sparks,
As they illuminate all the darks.
With every zap, laughter ignites,
An underwater show of dazzling sights!

Shining Navigators of the Deep

Bubble-blowers in a glowing fleet,
Guiding mischief with wiggling feet.
Each fish a captain, snappy and spry,
Plotting adventures where giggles fly.

With shiny maps made of squid and ink,
They plot their travels, and never blink.
A treasure chest filled with old jokes,
Waiting to share with curious folks.

As they navigate in a wiggly line,
With flashing smiles that truly shine.
They gather tales from the seas so wide,
Capturing laughter like the moon's gentle tide.

From coral canyons to kelp forests green,
Their joyful shenanigans, quite the scene.
Every flip, every gleam, a burst of cheer,
In the playful depths, it's all sincere!

The Glow of Forgotten Waters

In shadows deep where the old tales flow,
Glowfish giggle in a whimsical show.
They tickle the current with every flick,
Making waves and laughter, a playful trick.

Forgotten treasures, old as can be,
Glow with whimsy, oh can't you see?
Octopuses juggling shiny old rocks,
As seahorses dance in their fancy frocks.

In abysmal nooks of playful frights,
Fish throw parties on moonlit nights.
Grinning deep with the ocean's glee,
Where glowing creatures swim wild and free.

The currents hum laughter, soft and bright,
Enveloping all in sheer delight.
So join the jesters, come dive and play,
In these forgotten waters, every day!

www.ingramcontent.com/pod-product-compliance
Lightning Source LLC
Chambersburg PA
CBHW060142230426
43661CB00003B/531